# Tender In My 20's

words from my early twenties written by the sea meant for the soul

Summer Dupree

BookLeaf Publishing
India | USA | UK

Made with ❤ on the BookLeaf Publishing Platform
www.bookleafpub.in
www.bookleafpub.com

# Dedication

for the ones learning how to love themselves again.
for the ones healing quietly.
for the ones still blooming—this is for you.

# Preface

This book is a collection of pieces from all the versions of
me I've met along the way of my early twenties—
the girl who tried to carry it all, the nostalgic dreamer,
the one learning how to let go,
and the one learning how to hold herself gently.
These poems were written in quiet moments,
in car rides and beach days,
in between longing and laughter,
in the deep end of grief and the first breath of healing.
They are about becoming—
slowly, imperfectly, beautifully.
They are about the ache of choosing yourself,
the softness that follows sorrow,
and the light that always finds a way back in.
If you're holding this book,
I hope it feels like a friend.
I hope it reminds you that you're allowed to feel
everything
and still believe in your own becoming.
Here's to the growing, glowing, ever-changing you

# Acknowledgements

To the people who held space for me while I grew—
thank you.
To those who stayed, and to those who left—you were all
part of this.
To every friend who read a poem, encouraged me, or
simply listened—your love lives in these pages.
To the versions of myself that wrote these poems—tired,
tender, confused, soft, blooming—thank you for feeling
so deeply. You made this real.
To the ocean, for always reminding me who I am.
To the sun, for coming back every morning.
And to you, reader—thank you for holding these words
with care. I hope something in them made you feel a
little more seen.
This book is what happens when you don't give up on
yourself.

# 1. August

& when our eyes met for the first time
on that late August night, something shifted.
the air changed –
like the silence between waves
just before the tide turns.
it was as if our souls remembered
what our bodies had not yet touched–
a softness,
a gravity.
we both felt it,
that quiet, electric pull,
as if the universe whispered,
*"you've been here before."*
like a reconnection,
like the stars were realigning
just to witness this moment.
your laugh unlocked something in me–
something I didn't know I'd sealed.
I noticed the way your hands danced when you talked,
the one freckle just beneath your left eye darker than the

others,
how you said my name like a secret.
a knowing.
not loud, not urgent—
but deep.
bone-deep.
as if love didn't need time
to make itself known.

# 2. I Hate the Sunset Tonight

i hate the sunset tonight
because the colors remind me of your soul—
golden, fiery,
always slipping just out of reach.
i hate the sunset tonight
and every night since you left,
because all i can think of
is how we used to sit side by side
in quiet reverence, wine in hand,
shoulders touching
like we were made to fit.
those skies felt endless—
and so did we.
i used to map out our lives
between sips of pinot and stolen glances,
imagining the years stretching ahead of us
like the horizon line:
blurry, but beautiful.
full of late-night whispers
under tangled sheets,

spontaneous road trips
with no plans but each other,
sunday morning coffee
kisses between sips,
your sleepy smile pressed into my neck.
i saw forever in you.
in the way your eyes held stories
i never got to finish reading.
in the way time stopped
when you looked at me
like i was your whole world.
and now,
the sky still burns with color—
but without you,
it just feels like ash.

# 3. Inevitable

i love the way sunlight
peeks through the clouds
just to touch the earth—
as if it can't help itself,
can't stay away.
just like my thoughts of you.
they come uninvited,
but never unwelcome.
inevitable.
like muscle memory,
or gravity,
or the ache you left behind.
just like my hands
could never stay off you—
always needing
to feel the heat of your skin
beneath my fingertips,
tracing your outline,
mapping the shape of us
in the dark.

i memorized every inch of you
like scripture.
like a prayer
i wasn't supposed to say out loud.
and even if i knew
you'd burn me to the bone—
i would still choose
to walk into the flame,
over
and over,
until all that was left of me
was light.

# 4. Dream Realm

sometimes when i close my eyes
i enter the same dream—
a realm stitched from mist
and memory,
where time folds like silk
and you are always waiting.
sometimes, you're by the ocean,
standing ankle-deep in a tide
that never reaches me.
sometimes, we're in the living room,
but the walls breathe,
and the light hums like it knows
what i refuse to say aloud.
your face is always clear.
your voice, softer than the wind.
you never age here.
neither do i.
i try to speak
but the words come out in colors.
you smile,

like you understand anyway.
i reach for you—
always,
i reach.
and just before our hands meet,
the world begins to blur.
i wake up
with the shape of you
still resting on my chest,
as if you never left.
as if you only live
in my dreams now.

# 5. Tracing Ghosts with my Fingers

i still reach for you in the quiet ways—
when a song plays that once was the theme of our lives,
or i hear someone talking references from your favorite show
or i catch my reflection mid-laugh
and remember the way we would laugh so hard we would cry
you were there for all my becoming.
through the years i shapeshifted,
shedding skins, cutting my hair,
breaking and rebuilding myself again.
and you never flinched.
you held my hand like it was the most natural thing—
to grow and stay close.
you loved every version of me
until you didn't.
and i still don't know
how to unwrite the story where our friendship lasted a lifetime

maybe we were only meant to grow together for a short
time
but damn
it does not take away the pain of mourning someone
who is very much still alive

# 6. My Heart Screaming for Air

there was a time
i couldn't breathe without breaking.
grief stacked itself on my chest–
names i used to say daily now echo in silence
people who i thought were forever
but now I'm left with questions i still cannot answer
and love–
even that began to ache,
like wearing a sweater that no longer fit
but still smelled like home.
i wanted to feel normal again.
just one full breath.
just one day without carrying
the weight of conversations that never came,
the silence of people who once knew everything.
i begged the universe
for lightness.
for peace.
for anything that didn't feel like drowning.

and then,
one day,
i woke up and realized:
i made it.
my heart,
bruised but beating,
still knew how to laugh in the sunlight.
i still knew how to love,
how to dance barefoot in the kitchen,
how to be whole
without the people who left.
this is not the version of life i imagined—
but it's the one i survived for.
and finally,
i can breathe.

# 7. Softness in the Cracks

on the days
i no longer want to exist,
i remind myself–
of the way sunlight
caresses my skin,
how rain smells
on a warm spring afternoon,
a hug from my mother
that makes me feel
so safe
i almost cry.
the sound of my grandmother's laughter
echoing down the hall,
the rich smell of coffee
in the stillness of morning.
animal cuddles.
my best friend's smile.
belly laughs
that make you forget the weight of everything.
tea shared with someone

who sees you
as you are.
and in these moments,
i remember:
there is still so much
to live for.

# 8. A Conversation with My Angels

i find myself clinging
to the moments in front of me—
knuckles turning white
from holding on so tightly,
as if presence could be preserved
with enough effort.
i try to memorize
every detail of *right now.*
the soft curve of my mother's smile,
the way the lines on her face deepen
with each expression—
etched stories i never want to forget.
i trace them with my eyes
like scripture,
knowing i'll never get this time back.
and that knowing—
is both beautiful
and unbearable.
beautiful,

that i get to live this moment at all.
unsettling,
that it's already slipping away.
it's like i feel nostalgia
before the moment is even over.
like my heart is mourning
in real-time.
and no matter how tightly i grip it,
time runs through my fingers
like water in a cupped hand—
impossible to keep,
but sacred all the same.

# 9. Growing Pains

i am 10 years old.
i spent the day at my grandma's,
swimming in her pool,
eating fresh strawberries
and the salad she made with her hands—
always with too much olive oil
and love.
in the late afternoon,
the frogs would begin to sing.
the air smelled like chlorine and cut grass,
and nothing mattered
but how many times i could do a handstand
before dinner.
time didn't exist back then.
not really.
just sunburnt shoulders
and juice-stained smiles.
i didn't worry about aging,
about goals,
or running out of time.

i watched the way my grandma laughed
with her whole chest,
the lines around her eyes softening
every time she looked at me.
i didn't know those lines meant age.
i just thought they meant love.
but somewhere along the way,
the world handed me a clock
and called it womanhood.
society taught me to fear aging—
to believe that turning 26
meant i was running out of time,
instead of realizing
that maybe life
is just now beginning.

# 10. No Wrong Way

sometimes,
i mourn the lives i didn't choose.
the ones i almost lived.
the people i almost became.
there are versions of me
scattered like seashells
on paths i never took—
and sometimes,
i feel the weight of what could have been.
but i'm learning:
there are no wrong roads.
just different winds.
just different skies.
and every time i chose,
even when it felt like breaking,
something sacred grew in the space i stepped into.
it's okay to grieve the "what ifs."
but i don't have to live inside them.
this life,
this moment,

this breath—
it is not a mistake.
so i choose to be here.
not where i thought i'd be.
not where it might have been softer.
but here—
with both hands open.
and that,
i think,
is enough.

# 11. The things I Buried

i recently uncovered something about myself;
i am so afraid of letting myself fully enjoy something,
because what if it doesn't last?
—nothing ever lasts.
but lately,
i've been learning to hold joy with open hands,
letting it land gently
like a bird on my shoulder—
never mine to keep,
but beautiful while it's here.
maybe some moments are meant to be temporary,
not to teach us loss,
but presence.
and i want to be here for the good parts—
even if they're temporary
especially because they're temporary.

# 12. Sunlight Between my Ribs

today is a good day.
i drank matcha
and sat under the sun—
let it kiss my skin
while i remembered how to breathe.
today is a good day.
i collected shells by the shore,
held small pieces of the ocean
in my palms
like tiny treasures.
today is a good day.
i brought my soul dog
to watch the sky turn pink,
and we both sat still
like we understood
how sacred that was.
today is a good day.
i ate food that nourished my body
and tasted like self care

i gave thanks.
today is a good day.
and i'm learning
to notice when it is.

# 13. Softly, from afar

i hope it's nice where you are.
i hope it's your favorite weather
and you are enjoying a cup of tea.
we don't speak now,
and maybe that's what peace looks like.
but sometimes, when the sky is just the right color,
i still send you silent wishes,
tucked between the clouds.

# 14. Love that Feels Like Breathing

she cracked open my chest and made a home within my heart,
planting flowers and opening the curtains for sunlight to pour in.
loving her is like breathing oxygen, second nature.
she grounds me with a touch when my mind runs wild.
she remembers my coffee order,
and leaves notes on the mirror
she sings in the car with the windows down,
always reaching for my hand at red lights.
and when she looks at me—
really looks—
it's like the whole world softens.
she makes me feel like sunset skies on an endless day.

# 15. Permission to Love

life can sometimes feel suffocating
but the only thing i'd want to drown in
is the taste of your lips on mine—
i'd forget to come up for air,
and what a sweet surrender it would be
to give my breath away for you.
i'd give you so much more than my breath—
i'd give you the ache in my chest
and the hope stitched between each heartbeat.
i'd give you my quietest thoughts,
the ones i never say out loud.
i'd give you every version of me—
the soft, the shattered,
the blooming.
and even if you never ask,
i'd still give.
because loving you
never needed permission

# 16. Ocean Deep

i look into her eyes
and i feel a mix of emotions,
like i'm floating in the ocean
while also sinking so deep.
her gaze holds galaxies
and storms,
a calm i crave
and a chaos i don't know how to survive.
being with her is like forgetting how to swim
and not wanting to remember—
letting the tide take me
wherever she goes.
i don’t know if she’s my anchor
or the current pulling me under.
all i know is
i don’t want to look away.

# 17. Fire in My Fingertips

you've been sitting at the edge of my life
like a sunset i kept watching
but never believed i could walk toward.
you smell like saltwater and soft mornings.
you sound like laughter i don't apologize for.
you feel like a body unclenched–
a life without deadlines,
a silence that doesn't punish.
i thought of you often
between clinicals and cramming,
in the still moments between exams
and breakdowns i called "fine."
you always waited–
quiet, patient,
unbothered by how long it took.
i was scared of you.
i still am.
but i'm more scared
of who i'm becoming
when i forget to rest,

when i live only to keep up.
so if i whisper,
will you still come?
if i leave the to-do list unfinished,
if i slip off the weight i've been wearing,
if i cry from exhaustion as i walk toward you—
will you still open your arms?
because i want to be brave.
i want to come home to myself.
i want to stop trading peace
for productivity.
permission
for presence.
if you're listening—
please wait just a little longer.
i'm almost free.
i'm almost ready.
*-poem to life after grad school*

# 18. The Ocean in My Chest

there's a tide in me
that doesn't want to stay still.
it rises with the sun,
crashes against the bones that try to hold it in.
i used to think my depth was a burden—
too much emotion,
too many questions,
a heart that wanted everything
all at once.
but now—
i let it pull me.
i chase the warmth,
run toward the light
barefoot and breathless.
there is an ocean in my chest
and it's not here to drown me.
it's here to carry me—
to places i've never been,
to people who feel like sunlight,
to versions of myself

i haven't even met yet.
i was never meant to stay on the shore.
i was made to touch the horizon,
to laugh with salt on my lips,
to live wide open—
wild and warm
and full of feeling

# 19. Golden Hour Skin

i love going to watch the sunrise—
to be among the clouds
before the earth wakes up.
when the light begins to rise,
it touches my skin
like it knows my name.
i bask in the warmth,
and my soul lights up,
like it's been waiting all along.
this—
this is the meaning of it all.
how silly to have forgotten,
to get caught in the noise and rush,
to care at all what others thought of me
to shrink myself for spaces
that were never mine to fit
but here,
bathed in honeyed light,
i just exist—
wild,

open,
glowing.
and maybe that's enough.
maybe i was always enough.
the sun just reminded me.

# 20. Love Letter to Myself

25 feels like
being more gentle with myself.
like exhaling the pressure,
softening the edges,
choosing presence over perfection.
it feels like being okay
with being perceived—
because life isn't that serious anyway.
like dancing without looking around.
laughing with my whole body.
wearing what makes me feel like art.
25 feels like joy.
like playfulness returning
after years of hiding.
like awe in the little things—
sunlight through curtains,
good music in the car,
this one precious life.
it feels like trusting myself
more than ever before,

and trusting the universe, too—
knowing she's always had my back.
25 feels like
i've finally befriended
all the versions of me
i used to run from.
and now,
we sit together in peace

# 21. The Softest Version of Me

the softest version of me
smells like saltwater and sunscreen.
she wakes up with tangled hair,
walks barefoot through her thoughts,
and lets the ocean kiss her ankles
like it's saying, *you made it.*
she doesn't rush.
she lets the day hold her gently—
coffee in one hand,
freedom in the other.
she sings with the windows down,
collects seashells like memories,
laughs without shrinking,
and forgives herself out loud.
she lets the tide take what it must.
lets joy rush in like waves.
lets her body rest in sunlight
without asking if she's earned it.
she tries things she's bad at

just to feel alive,
paints without worrying if it's good,
writes poetry that no one else needs to understand.
she is soft, not fragile.
gentle, not quiet.
a storm and a still sea—
all in one.
and she is enough—
not because she chased perfection,
but because she finally came home to herself.
-and maybe, you will too

www.ingramcontent.com/pod-product-compliance
Lightning Source LLC
Chambersburg PA
CBHW051745130826
49812CB00033B/1011